W9-AUY-740

# Folk Songs

# North American Folklore

Children's Folklore
Christmas and Santa Claus Folklore
Contemporary Folklore
Ethnic Folklore
Family Folklore
Firefighters' Folklore
Folk Arts and Crafts
Folk Customs
Folk Dance
Folk Fashion
Folk Festivals
Folk Games
Folk Medicine
Folk Music
Folk Proverbs and Riddles
Folk Religion
Folk Songs
Folk Speech
Folk Tales and Legends
Food Folklore
Regional Folklore

## North American Folklore

# Folk Songs

BY PETER SIELING

Mason Crest Publishers

Mason Crest Publishers Inc.
370 Reed Road
Broomall, Pennsylvania 19008
(866) MCP-BOOK (toll free)
www.masoncrest.com

First printing
1 2 3 4 5 6 7 8 9 10
Library of Congress Cataloging-in-Publication Data on file at the Library of Congress.
ISBN 1-59084-344-4
      1-59084-328-2 (series)

Design by Lori Holland.
Composition by Bytheway Publishing Services, Binghamton, New York.
Cover design by Joe Gilmore.
Printed and bound in the Hashemite Kingdom of Jordan.

**Picture credits:**
Comstock: p. 44
Corbis: p. 54
Corel: pp. 6, 32, 60, 62
J. Rowe: pp. 12, 24, 25, 27, 31, 34, 37, 40, 46, 70, 74, 76, 78, 83, 87, 89, 90, 92, 96, 98, 100
Cover: "Singing the Old Oaken Bucket" by J. F. Kernan © 1923 SEPS: Licensed by Curtis Publishing, Indianapolis, IN. www.curtispublishing.com

# Contents

Folklore grows from long-ago
seeds. Just as an acorn sends
down roots even as it shoots up
leaves across the sky, folklore is
rooted deeply in the past and
yet still lives and grows today.
It spreads through our modern
world with branches as wide
and sturdy as any oak's;
it grounds us in yesterday even
as it helps us make sense of
both the present and the future.

# Introduction

by Dr. Alan Jabbour

WHAT DO A TALE, a joke, a fiddle tune, a quilt, a jig, a game of jacks, a saint's day procession, a snake fence, and a Halloween costume have in common? Not much, at first glance, but all these forms of human creativity are part of a zone of our cultural life and experience that we sometimes call "folklore."

The word "folklore" means the cultural traditions that are learned and passed along by ordinary people as part of the fabric of their lives and culture. Folklore may be passed along in verbal form, like the urban legend that we hear about from friends who assure us that it really happened to a friend of their cousin. Or it may be tunes or dance steps we pick up on the block, or ways of shaping things to use or admire out of materials readily available to us, like that quilt our aunt made. Often we acquire folklore without even fully realizing where or how we learned it.

Though we might imagine that the word "folklore" refers to cultural traditions from far away or long ago, we actually use and enjoy folklore as part of our own daily lives. It is often ordinary, yet we often remember and prize it because it seems somehow very special. Folklore is culture we share with others in our communities, and we build our identities through the sharing. Our first shared identity is family identity, and family folklore such as shared meals or prayers or songs helps us develop a sense of belonging. But as we grow older we learn to belong to other groups as well. Our identities may be ethnic, religious, occupational, or regional—or all of these, since no one has only one cultural identity. But in every case, the identity is anchored and strengthened by a variety of cultural traditions in which we participate and share with our neighbors. We feel the threads of connection with people we know, but the threads extend far beyond our own immediate communities. In a real sense, they connect us in one way or another to the world.

Folklore possesses features by which we distinguish ourselves from each other. A certain dance step may be African American, or a certain story urban, or a certain hymn Protestant, or a certain food preparation Cajun. Folklore can distinguish us, but at the same time it is one of the best ways we introduce ourselves to each other. We learn about new ethnic groups on the North American landscape by sampling their cuisine, and we enthusiastically adopt musical ideas from other communities. Stories, songs, and visual designs move from group to group, enriching all people in the process. Folklore thus is both a sign of identity, experienced as a special marker of our special groups, and at the same time a cultural coin that is well spent by sharing with others beyond our group boundaries.

Folklore is usually learned informally. Somebody, somewhere, taught us that jump rope rhyme we know, but we may have trouble remembering just where we got it, and it probably wasn't in a book that was assigned as homework. Our world has a domain of formal knowledge, but folklore is a domain of knowledge and culture that is learned by sharing and imitation rather than formal instruction. We can study it formally—that's what we are doing now!—but its natural arena is in the informal, person-to-person fabric of our lives.

Not all culture is folklore. Classical music, art sculpture, or great novels are forms of high art that may contain folklore but are not themselves folklore. Popular music or art may be built on folklore themes and traditions, but it addresses a much wider and more diverse audience than folk music or folk art. But even in the world of popular and mass culture, folklore keeps popping up around the margins. E-mail is not folklore—but an e-mail smile is. And college football is not folklore—but the wave we do at the stadium is.

This series of volumes explores the many faces of folklore throughout the North American continent. By illuminating the many aspects of folklore in our lives, we hope to help readers of the series to appreciate more fully the richness of the cultural fabric they either possess already or can easily encounter as they interact with their North American neighbors.

*Before the days of television, singing was once a family entertainment.*

# ONE

# Why Do We Sing?
## The Meaning of Song

*Bird song has inspired human beings for thousands of years.*

HUMANS LOVE to find patterns. One of the amazing things that sets humankind apart from the animals is the ability to perceive shape, meaning, and beauty in the midst of life's circumstances. We notice the shape of a face on a rock cliff. We hear wind whispering through spruce needles. The spring chorus frogs sing, and a man whistles, imitating the tremolo effect and adding extra runs and trills. Two chickadees sing their spring song in two different keys, and the ragtime composer, Scott Joplin, turns it into *Bethena, a Concert Waltz*. We turn sound and rhythm into music and fill the monotony of our lives with music and art.

Through all history we have sung for every reason imaginable. Hymns express love and adoration of our Creator. Blues express our sadness and sorrow at life's woes. Love songs express the romantic feelings we have for members of the opposite sex. We sing about our dull boring work—and work suddenly seems worth doing. We sing songs about historic events "that we may never forget," as a memorial, a way to **capsulate** the memory and pass it on to our children (and their children). Every shade of human emotion is covered by music. Both good and bad experiences are somehow enriched by converting them into song. Songs help us remember and make sense of life's experiences.

Slowly, over the last hundred years, new forms of music have tried to crowd out singing. It is hard to coax a tune out of your own lips when you can turn on the radio and hear professional voices that make yours sound like a frog with a horse in its throat. People sing less now, but listen to more music than ever.

Singing is like the bluebird. When the starling was introduced from Europe to America, it aggressively took over the bluebirds' nesting sites. That doesn't make the starling an evil bird. It eats lots of bugs. But the bluebird must now struggle for existence (and with people's help, bluebirds are making a comeback). In a similar way, recorded music has nearly replaced its shy cousin, homemade music. Recorded music isn't evil, but its **ubiquitous** nature crowds out singing.

## DATING OF FOLK SONGS

Since folk songs are passed around orally and changed with each singer, the process of determining the date is challenging. Many songs provide clues, which help musical sleuths in their investigation.

1. Since songs were a way of distributing news, many folk songs often start out with the date.
2. Old songs sometimes contain obsolete words or words that are no longer in common usage. These words can be compared with songs or literature of the same area and with a known date.
3. Old songs sometimes refer to inventions or modes of travel common to their era. In the case of "modern" inventions of the times, the standard words may not even be in use. A 1907 reference to "a birdman perched on a hill north of

# WHO IS ALAN LOMAX?

Anyone interested in folk music will find the name Alan Lomax appearing in book after book on the subject of folk music. He is arguably the most influential person in the folk music field as a folklorist, recordist, and author. Born in Austin, Texas in 1915, he began working with his father, John Lomax, to record folk songs for the Library of Congress. Together, father and son created thousands of field recordings of folk musicians throughout the United States. In addition to recording, they published a series of folk music collections, including *American Ballads and Folk Songs*.

In 1937, Alan Lomax became the director of the Archive of American Folk Song at the Library of Congress. By 1939, he was producing a national radio series for CBS. The program provided national exposure to local folk musicians such as Woody Guthrie, Leadbelly, Aunt Molly Jackson, Josh White, the Golden Gate Quartet, Burl Ives, and Pete Seeger.

Lomax revolutionized folk music by recording it. He made technology available to people who still passed their music on by word of mouth. In addition he promoted and popularized musical styles unknown in other parts of the country. He introduced people to blues and ballads, cajun and calypso. He carried his tape recorder into the backwoods and backwaters of America, recording music never heard before outside the region.

He popularized such folk icons as Jelly Roll Morton, Muddy Waters, Memphis Slim, Big Bill Broonzy, and Sonny Boy Williamson. After he left the Library of Congress, he continued to make field trips and recorded more music, expanding to cover Europe and folk songs of the whole world.

Throughout his life he continued to record and publish books, articles, films, and television programs. When the Voyager space probe was sent toward the very edge of the Universe, Lomax made sure recordings of Blind Willie Johnson and Louis Armstrong, Native American chants, and other ethnic music was sent along, spreading Earth folk songs to alien worlds. When computer technology made it possible, he developed a "global jukebox," featuring all the folk song styles of the world.

Lomax's philosophy, the principal of cultural equity, means that in expression, all peoples are equal. To that end, musical expression ought to be recorded and shared with others. In an age of cultural homogenization, when people all over the world are blending and merging toward one world culture, the recording of folk songs helps preserve and affirm diversity.

town" sounds peculiar to modern ears. We would say a pilot landed an airplane on a hill north of town.

4. Older songs may refer to customs no longer practiced (for example, kings and nobility or duels).

5. The modal scale of a song may vary with the time and location.

6. Musical styles can indicate an era. For instance, a waltz or polka style establishes a relatively narrow time frame and location for the song.

7. Old newspapers sometimes published poetry that then became folk music because of its popularity. By reading old newspapers, it is possible to sometimes find an author and date for what has become a folk song.

8. Songs can sometimes be traced back to their country of origin.

Recorded music can never replace singing completely. Like the television, it lacks active participation and the three dimensions of a live singer. As soon as listeners forget they are a passive listener, they will find themselves singing along with the radio.

Why do we sing? Because music is there inside us. It's been there since the first Man and the first Woman saw a sunset, shaped a tool out of stone, or formed a relationship—and it overflows. It's a way we express our emotions; it's a way we shape our experiences into patterns and rhythms. It gives us joy. And it's just plain fun.

*"The Arkansas Traveler"*

Sometimes another type of song ends up as a folk song. For instance, the official song of Arkansas was immensely popular in the 1800s. Today, the melody is still popular; although most people may not know its name, virtually every person in America knows it.

# THE ARKANSAS TRAVELER

Oh, once upon a time in Arkansas,
An old man sat in his little cabin door,
And he fiddled at a tune that he liked to hear,
A jolly old tune that he played by ear,
It was raining hard but the fiddler didn't care
He sawed away at the popular air,
though his roof tree leaked like a waterfall
That didn't seem to bother the man at all.

A traveler was riding by that day
And stopped to hear him a fiddling away
The cabin was afloat and his feet were wet,
But still the old man didn't seem to fret.
So the stranger said, "Now, the way it seems to me,
You'd better mend your roof," said he.
But the old man said as he played away,
"I couldn't mend it now, it's a rainy day."

The traveler replied, "That's all quite true,
But this, I think, is the thing for you to do-
Get busy on a day that is fair and bright,
Then patch the old roof till it's good and tight."
But the old man kept on a-playing at his reel,
And tapped the ground with his leathery heel.
"Get along," said he, "for you give me a pain,
My cabin never leaks when it doesn't rain!"

*Harvest was hard work before the days of machinery; singing made the work go faster.*

# TWO

# Work and Occupational Songs
## The Rhythm of Routine

*Many songs were inspired by the sailors' life; sea shanteys were songs whose beat came from the rhythm of the sailors' work.*

$S$ONGS EXPRESS PEOPLES' experiences. The average worker spends a half to two-thirds of his or her waking hours working. In the old days, nearly all a person's waking hours were at work. It is not surprising that so many folk songs were work songs.

Songs reflected the types of labor people performed. Generally the harsher the work, the more music grew out of it. You don't hear many songs about attorneys or accounting: *"I've been workin' on the cal-culator, all the livelong day. . ."* You do hear songs about mining coal, logging, cattle herding, and long haul trucking. These workers worked hard with their bodies—but meanwhile, their minds apparently craved creative expression.

People in authority don't seem to sing about their experience as much as the workers under them do. Underdogs just seem to need to express their rebellion and frustration and sorrow in song. Maybe it's a way of affirming their identities and human dignity. Maybe it's a way of taking hope even in the midst of what feels like oppression.

Last of all, singing improves group efficiency. By providing a rhythm, it helps workers coordinate their movements. Like a drill sargeant barking out marching steps, song ensures that a body of laborers moves to the same beat. And if it adds a sense of joy and hope to the process, so much the better.

## SLAVERY

The worst form of oppression—slavery—produced perhaps the richest music of all. The constant singing of the slaves was often

*When the folklorist collected this African American work song, the singer told him the song wasn't a work song but an "ain't workin' song."*

Eighteen hundred and ninety-one,
'Fore I workses, I'd ruther be hung.

Eighteen hundred and ninety-two
Me a' old worksy, we done been through.

Eighteen hundred and ninety-three,
Me and old worksy, we can't agree.

Eighteen hundred and ninety-four,
I lef' old worksy standin' at the workhouse door.

Eighteen hundred and ninety-five,
'Fore I workses, I be bad lie.

Eighteen hundred and ninety-six,
Me an' old worksies, we business to fix.

Eighteen hundred and ninety-seven,
Work killed my brother and sent him to heaven.

Eighteen hundred and ninety-eight,
I lef' old worksy standin' at the workhouse gate.

Eighteen hundred and ninety-nine,
I outrun worksy, and I left him behind.
Because I never like to work-a nohow.

From *Our Singing Country*, collected and compiled by John A. Lomax and Alan Lomax (Mineola, N.Y.: Dover, 2000), pp. 389–390.

interpreted as a sign that the slaves were a happy-go-lucky group of contented folks. According to Frederick Douglass, however, nothing could have been further from the truth. Slaves sang most when they were unhappy. Their singing relieved sorrow, the way tears relieve an aching heart.

The slaves at work were always singing. Sometimes the songs were hymns looking forward to a better life. Sometimes the songs provided a rhythm to the work. Flailing rice, spinning, weaving, hoeing sweet potatoes, loading and unloading steamboats required repetitive movements. In all cases, the songs added a little color to a drab and hard existence.

Slaves' masters liked to hear whistling and singing as long as the slaves did not sing slow songs. The masters felt fast songs made the work go faster, so they could squeeze more work out of the slaves. And noisy slaves sounded content. The silent sullen ones made slaveholders uneasy, because they never knew what they might be planning. It was also easier to track loud singing slaves in the fields of tall crops, where the overseers could follow their progress in the harvest as they moved back and forth through the field.

> Working all day,
> And part of the night,
> And up before the morning light.
> When will Jehovah hear our cry,
> And free the sons of Africa?

Some work songs told stories that may have been based on actual events, as this one does:

Oh, bad man Lazarus,
Oh, bad man Lazarus,
He broke in the commissary.
Lord, he broke in the commissary.

He been paid off,
He been paid off,
Lord, Lord, Lord,
He been paid off.

Commissary man,
Commissary man,
He jump out the commissary window,
Lord, he jump out the commissary window.

Oh, bring him back,
Lord, bring him back,
Lord, Lord, Lord,
Bring him back.

Well, the sheriff spied poor Lazarus,
Well, the sheriff spied poor Lazarus,
Lord, sheriff spied poor Lazarus,
Way between Bald Mountain.

They blowed him down,
Well, they blowed him down,
Well, Lord, Lord,
They blowed him down.

They shot poor Lazarus,
Lord, they shot poor Lazarus,

Lord, they shot poor Lazarus,
With a great big number.

They goin' to bury poor Lazarus,
Lord, they goin' to bury poor Lazarus,
They going to bury poor Lazarus,
Half past nine.

If the song seems to go forever (and I've left out several stanzas), remember that the work it accompanied went on forever too.

## MOVING FREIGHT

After love songs and religious hymns, there may be more songs about shipping freight than anything else. You may never have realized that before because more romantic-sounding subjects often disguised the subject. But songs of the sea are all about shipping goods from one place to another by water, whether the goods be molasses, lumber, spices, or iron ore. Even lowly canal barges have their large share of songs. A large body of music celebrates trains, whose primary purpose was to deliver goods over land. Cowboys herd cattle hundreds of miles to market, and they too have plenty of folk songs to call their own. (Chapter six deals in part with cowboy songs, and chapter seven focuses on railroad songs.) Modern folk songs are still written about truckers. "Looks like we got us a CONVOY!" Who would have thought such a mundane topic would prove to be so musically inspiring?

The reason for the huge *repertoire* of "freight" songs comes from the nature of the job. A fellow has a lot of time to think on road, rail, or sea. He is alone or with other lonely men and away from home for days, weeks, or even years. Long hours, loneliness, and dreary monotony seem to work together to force music out of a person.

## Wagoners' Songs

Wagoners were the first truckers. Instead of hauling freight with 18-wheel diesel Mack or Peterbilt tractor trailers, wagoners drove horses and wagons over the rutted dirt roads, pushing west with the pioneers, bringing crops east and supplies back west. Singing passed the time. One of the best-known old wagoners' songs is still well known today. (Most people also know the tune with the title "On Top of Spaghetti.")

On top of old Smoky,
All covered with snow,
I lost my true lover
By courting too slow.

Courting's a pleasure,
Parting's a grief,
And a false-hearted lover
Is worse than a thief.

They'll hug you and kiss you,
And tell you more lies
Than the cross ties on the railroad
Or the stars in the skies.

A thief he will rob you
And take all you have,
But a false-hearted lover
Will send you to your grave.

The grave will only decay you,
And turn you to dust.

Not one girl in a hundred
A poor boy can trust.

The following less common verses of the song reveal the wagoners' distrust of women:

It's raining, it's hailing,
The moon gives no light,
Your horses can't travel
This dark lonesome night.

Go put up your horses,
Feed them some hay.
Come sit down here beside me,
As long as your stay.

## Boating and Shipping

Hardly anything is more monotonous and repetitive than rowing. In the early 1800s, travelers by boat might find themselves among the rowers. The leader would sing out in time to the oars, and the others would answer with the chorus. For instance:

We are going down to Georgia, boys,
Aye, aye.
To see the pretty girls, boys.
Yoe, Yoe.
We'll give 'em a pint of brandy, boys
Aye, aye.
And a hearty kiss, besides, boys.
Yoe, you. . .

*Winding the capstan.*

The song goes on and on. The leader makes up the words as he goes. The tune is somewhat monotonous, like the labor, but the song keeps up a rhythm to the work, improving the entire group's efficiency.

## Sea Shanteys

In the days of the Phoenician sailors and later the Vikings, the anchor was dropped and pulled up hand over hand by a group of sailors. As ships grew in size, so did the anchor and line to which it was attached. The capstan allowed men to haul up a bigger anchor. It was built like a large winch, a spool with poles like spokes. The sailors put their weight into the spokes and wound the anchor cable up. The motions of winding the capstan were jerky, and the chanteys or "shanties" match with a jerky rhythm or their own.

# LUMBERJACKS

The life of a lumberjack was hard and often short. He spent the winter cutting trees and *sledging* them to the river. With the spring thaw, the river rose and the logs were pushed into the river to float downstream to the mills. Along the way, logs inevitably wedged against the banks, forming huge logjams. It was the job of one or

# BLOW THE MAN DOWN

Popeye fans know this classic sea song or chantey. The words refer to a Quaker-owned shipping company, the Black Ball Line, the first line to provide regularly scheduled passenger transportation in the early 1800s. Kicking Jack Williams was a real captain. The sailors were not the cream of the crop. Many had never been to sea before. Discipline by flogging was common.

Come all ye young fellows that follow the sea,
To my way, hey, blow the man down,
And pray, pay attention and listen to me
Give me some time to blow the man down.

I'm a deep water sailor just in from Hong Kong,
To my way, hey, blow the man down,
If you'll give me some grog, I'll sing you a song,
Give me some time to blow the man down.

several men to climb out on the jam and locate the "key," the log that held up the rest. They pried it loose, then ran for their life over the floating logs to shore. Many didn't make it, and there are still old crosses at spots along the rivers where men lost their lives.

> Now a lumberjack's life is of short duration,
> Made up of low wages, hard work and bad rum,
> But the Bible says there is a hereafter,
> And the worst of your days, boys, is yet to come.

## HOUSEKEEPING SONGS

Male laborers weren't the only ones to make up songs about their work. Before the labor-saving conveniences of modern life such as vacuum cleaners and dishwashers, the housewife worked long hard hours. Washing, ironing, and cleaning were pure drudgery. The tasks were eased somewhat by slotting certain jobs into established days of the week. In other words, women did the same jobs on the same day. Mothers taught their work to their children in song, and this well-known children's song suggests the weekly cycle of work:

> Here we go 'round the mulberry bush,
> The mulberry bush, the mulberry bush,
> Here we go 'round the mulberry bush,
> So early in the morning.

> This is the way we wash our clothes,
> Wash our clothes, wash our clothes,
> This is the way we wash our clothes,
> So early Monday morning.

This is the way we iron our clothes,
Iron our clothes, iron our clothes,
This is the way we iron our clothes,
So early Tuesday morning.

This is the way we sweep the floor,
Sweep the floor, sweep the floor,
This is the way we sweep the floor,
So early Wednesday morning.

This is the way we mend our clothes,
Mend our clothes, mend our clothes,
This is the way we mend our clothes,
So early Thursday morning.

This is the way we clean the house,
Clean the house, clean the house,
This is the way we clean the house,
So early Friday morning.

This is the way we bake our bread,
Bake our bread, bake our bread,
This is the way we bake our bread,
So early Saturday morning.

This is the way we go to church,
Go to church, go to church,
This is the way we go to church,
So early Sunday morning.

*"Here We Go 'Round the Mulberry Bush"*

# CAPE COD SHANTEY

Cape Cod girls they have no combs,
Heave away, heave away.
They comb their hair with codfish bones,
We are bound for Australia!

CHORUS
Heave away my bully boys,
Heave away, heave away.
Heave away and don't you make a noise,
We are bound for Australia!

Cape Cod boys they have no sleds,
Heave away, heave away.
They slide down hill on codfish heads.
We are bound for Australia!

CHORUS

The daily division of labor was not purely **arbitrary**. Cleaning occurred on Friday and baking on Saturday because of the strict observance of the Sabbath; most of our ancestors did not work on Sunday if they could help it. Hardworking women could rest from their labor on Sunday. The house would still be clean from Friday, and the family ate the food cooked on Saturday.

# HARVEST SONGS

Long hard labor in the hot summer sun led to the rewards of all that plowing, hoeing, and weeding—still more hard labor and even longer hours of harvest work. The crops had to be brought in before bad weather ruined them, and people sang to keep up the frantic pace. They also played games to lighten the work. (For instance, corn shuckings were turned into fun by hiding a colored ear in the stack. The person who found the ear got to kiss the boy or girl of his or her choice.)

Corn shucking songs were common. These were usually call-and-response songs that continued as long as the work continued. The melody and rhythms were simple, and the leader often made up the words as he sang them. Corn songs mostly have not survived to the present, because they were made up on the spot and were never written down. One early recounting of a song of slaves at a corn husking describes a song something like this:

> Leader: I loves old Virginny!
> *Chorus: So ho! boys, so ho!*
> I love to shuck corn!
> *So ho! boys, so ho!*
> Now's cottonpicking time!
> *So ho! boys, so ho!*

# THE ERIE CANAL

The early 1800s saw the great network of canals crisscrossing the East. The most famous, the old Erie Canal, connected Buffalo and Albany in New York State. The canal opened the "West" with inexpensive transportation. Other branches connected other parts of the state to the main canal. Bargemen traveled up and down the canal towed by mules walking the bank. Passengers often rode the barges sitting on top. The bridges spanning the canal were just high enough for the barges to squeeze under. When the bargeman called out, "Low bridge!" the passengers ducked or found themselves swept off their seat by the bridge.

I've got an old mule and her name is Sal,
Fifteen miles on the Erie Canal.
She's a good old worker and a good old pal
Fifteen miles on the Erie Canal
We've hauled some barges in our day,
Filled with lumber, coal, and hay,
And we know every inch of the way
From Albany to Buffalo.

CHORUS
Low bridge, everybody down!
Low bridge for we're coming to a town
And you'll always know your neighbor, you'll always know your pal,
If you've ever navigated on the Erie Canal.

*"The Erie Canal"*

We'll make the money, boys!
*So ho! boys, so ho!*

On it goes, the leader making up lines as he goes for hours and hours. When one leader tires, another picks up the song and the chorus line changes.

Today corn is harvested and processed by machines. The corn songs have mostly disappeared except the few that were written down. The harvesters ride in air-conditioned tractor cabs listening to love songs on the radio.

*Romantic love has always inspired song.*

# THREE

# Love Songs
## The Joy and Sorrow of Romance

"Love is a funny thing, Shaped just like a lizard."

SONGS EXPRESS the heights and depths of human emotions. From the songs heard on the radio, however, you might think there was no other emotion than romantic love. You can't get away from love songs. You either sing along in a haze of romantic dreams—or it makes you want to plug your ears and gag.

Love songs can be categorized roughly into one or a combination of these subjects:

1. Boy is in love with girl but girl doesn't love boy (or girl is in love with boy but boy doesn't love girl).
2. Boy cheats on girl (or vice versa).
3. Boy dies doing something heroic for the girl (or vice versa).
4. My guy (or girl) is so cool . . . or neat, swell, rad, hot, whatever the popular adjective of the month is.
5. Boy and girl both love each other and everybody is happy.
6. Boy and girl hate each other and nobody is happy.
7. Boy is from the upper socioeconomic level and girl is from the lower socioeconomic level (or vice versa).
8. Boy kills girl, either accidentally or on purpose (or girl kills boy).
9. Boy is mourning deceased girlfriend or girl is mourning deceased boyfriend.

Memorize this list and you will know the theme of 98 percent of all music ever written for all time all over the world. Admittedly, however, men and women who fall in love and marry will spend a good portion of time together. If it is true love and they work as a team, they will have a joyful life whatever hardships may come. A bad marriage can lead to sorrow and pain (at least until divorce or death end the couple's misery). Songs arise out of either situation.

This deep and tender love song only makes sense only when you have experienced true love:

> Love is a funny thing,
> Shaped just like a lizard.
> Runs right up your backbone
> And nibbles at your gizzard.

One of the oldest love songs has many versions and can be traced as far back as the mid-sixteenth century. It fits the category of lovers from different socioeconomic levels (if you can stretch the definition of "lovers" just a little). The first verse illustrates the repeating structure of the rest of the verses:

> Mister Froggie went a-courting, and he did ride, mm-
>     hmm.
> Mister Froggie went a-courting, and he did ride, mm-
>     hmm.
> Mister Froggie went a-courting, and he did ride,
> A sword and a pistol by his side, mm-hmm.
>
> He went down to Missy Mousy's door, mm-hmm.
> He went down to Missy Mousy's door,
> Where he had been many times before, mm-hmm.
>
> "Missy Mousey are you within, mm-hmm?
> Missy Mousey are you within?"

*"Froggie Went A-Courting"*

"Yes kind sir, I sit and spin," mm-hmm. [Spin-
    ning refers to making yarn, not twirling.]

He took Missy Mouse upon his knee,
    mm-hmm.
He took Missy Mouse upon his knee,
Said, "Missy Mouse, will you marry me?"
    mm-hmm.

"Without my Uncle Rat's consent, mm-hmm.
Without my Uncle Rat's consent,
I wouldn't marry the president," mm-hmm.

Uncle Rat laughed and shook his fat sides, mm-hmm.
To think his niece would be a bride, mm-hmm.

When Uncle Rat gave his consent,
The weasel wrote the publishment.

Next came in was a bumblebee,
Danced a jig with a two-legged flea.

The owl did hoot, the birds they sang,
And through the woods the music rang.

Where will the wedding breakfast be?
Way down yonder in a hollow tree.

What will the wedding breakfast be?
Two green beans and a black eyed pea.

They all went sailing across the lake,
And got swallowed up by a big black snake.

There's bread and cheese upon the shelf,
If you want any more, you can sing it yourself.

This love song has it all—declaration of true love, interminable wedding preparations, and tragic death. It's a classic tale that shows how love and sorrow are intertwined!

In every grade at school, there seems to be one or two girls that attract boys like bees to honey. Boys fall madly, deeply, and "eternally" in love with them for no apparent reason. Eventually, you'll see these girls, arms folded across chest, looking off into space—while some poor boy sits slumped in discouragement. He can't figure out why this girl won't "go out" with him. There may be a half dozen other girls who think he's a perfectly nice boy. But he had to fall for the same finicky girl to whom a dozen other boys are sending notes and gifts.

This classic ballad is rooted in a similar experience. It is found throughout the Western world; various versions appear wherever English is spoken. It is the pathetic story of a young man who goes "gaga" over a particular girl, their tragic misunderstanding, and a legend of the rose and its thorns.

# BARBARA ALLEN

In Scarlet town where I was born,
There lived a fair maid dwellin',
Made every youth cry "well a day,"
And her name was Barbara Allen.

'Twas in the merry month of May,
When green buds were a swellin',
Sweet William on his death bed lay,
For the love of Barbara Allen.

He sent his servant to the town,
To the place where she was a-dwellin',
Cried, "Master bids you come to him,
If your name be Barbara Allen."

Then slowly, slowly she got up,
And slowly went she nigh him,
And when she pulled the curtains back,
Said, "Young man, I think you're dyin'."

"Oh yes I'm sick, I'm very sick,
And I never will be better,
Until I have the love on one,
The love of Barbara Allen."

"Oh, **ken** ye not in yonder town
In the place where you were a-dwellin',
You gave a toast to the ladies all,
But you slighted Barbara Allen."

"Oh yes, I ken, I ken it well,
In the place where I was a-dwellin',
I gave a toast to the ladies all,
But my love to Barbara Allen."

Then lightly tripped she down the stairs,
He trembled like an aspen.
'Tis vain, 'tis vain, my dear young man,
To pine for Barbara Allen.

She walked out in the green, green fields.
She heard his death bells knellin'.
And every stroke they seemed to say,
"Hard hearted Barbara Allen."

Her eyes looked east, her eyes looked
   west,
She saw the pale corpse comin'.
She cried, "Bearers, bearers put him
   down
That I may look upon him."

The more she looked, the more she
   grieved,
Until she busts out cryin'.
She cried, "Bearers, bearers take him
   off,
For I am now a-dyin'."

*"Barbara Allen"*

"Oh, Father go and dig my grave,
Go dig it deep and narrow.
Sweet William died for me today,
I'll die for him tomorrow."

They buried her in the old churchyard,
Sweet William's grave was nigh her,
And from his heart grew a red, red rose,
And from her heart a briar.

They grew and grew o'er the old church wall,
Till they couldn't grow no higher,
Until they tied a true lover's knot,
The red rose and the briar.

But maybe the most sentimental love song ever written in all of history is an Irish song sung to "Londonderry Air." It's also known as "Danny Boy," one of the most beautiful folk melodies ever composed.

Would God I were the tender apple blossom
That floats and falls from off the twisted bough,
To lie and faint within your silken bosom,
Within your silken bosom as that does now!

Or would I were a little burnished apple
For you to pluck me, gliding by so cold,
While sun and shade your robe of lawn will dapple,
Your robe of lawn and your hair's spun gold.

Yea, would to God I were among the roses
That lean to kiss you as you float between,

While on the lowest branch a bud uncloses,
A bud uncloses to touch you, Queen.

Nay, since you will not love, would I were growing
A happy daisy in the garden path;
That so your silver foot might press me going,
Might press me going even unto death!

Adolescence is a difficult time, especially when the opposite gender becomes interesting. Imagine living your life "up in the **holler**" with little chance to sharpen your social skills. That's the situation described in this song:

Johnson boys were raised in the
    ashes,
Didn't know how to court a maid,
Turn their backs and hide their faces,
Sight of a pretty girl makes 'em
    afraid.

Johnson boys they went a-courtin',
Coon Creek girls so pretty and sweet,
They couldn't make no conversation,
They didn't know where to put their feet.

Johnson boys'll never get married,
They'll stay single all their life,
They're too scared to pop the question,
Ain't no woman that'll be their wife.

The Coon Creek girls may be taunting the clumsy shy Johnsons now. In a couple years their tune changes:

> Have you heard the many stories
> Told by young and old with joy?
> Of the many deeds of daring
> That was done by the Johnson boys?
>
> Johnson boys were men of honor
> And knew how to kiss the maids,
> Hug and kiss them, call them "honey."
> Hop up pretty girls, don't be afraid.
>
> They were men of skill and courage
> And the sight was very far,
> They joined up in the country service
> In that awful Civil War.
>
> They were scouts in the rebel army
> And were known both far and wide,
> When the Yankees saw them coming
> They throw'd down their guns and hide.

Relationships between the sexes have always been fraught with excitement, tension, and misunderstanding. No wonder then that so many songs have been written on this subject!

*Religion is a rich source of folk songs.*

# FOUR

# Spirituals and Religious Songs
## Bound for Glory

*"Roll, Jordan, Roll"* is a folk song with both African American and English roots.

PRIOR TO THE Protestant reformation in the mid 1500s, many hymns were sung in Latin. This practice tended to separate ordinary people from their faith. Most people could neither read nor write, much less speak a second language.

Religious reformers of that age reconnected the people to their Christian faith by translating the Bible into the languages of the people. Hymns followed quickly. With their melody and meter, sacred songs were easy for illiterate people to learn. Early hymns were simply constructed with one note per syllable.

"Old Hundred" is perhaps the best known of these early hymns. Originally, the words came from Psalm 100 in the Bible. It is found in the Genevan Psalter of 1551 and is still sung every Sunday in traditional churches. It is often called "The Doxology," although there are many doxologies.

> Praise God from whom all blessings flow,
> Praise Him, all creatures here below.
> Praise Him above, ye heavenly host,
> Praise Father, Son, and Holy Ghost.

The new style of worship and expression of faith slowly reverted to a highly formalized style. By the 1700s, the established churches were controlled by the clergy, who were scholars of Greek and Latin; they were far removed from the concerns and troubles of common people. Religious expression was austere and formal.

In reaction to this formalism, John Wesley, an Anglican clergyman, preached outside the churches and cathedrals in open fields. He taught of individual faith through inner conviction of sin and repentance. His Methodist movement grew rapidly among the middle and lower classes. The Methodists expressed their faith musically by putting new words to popular tunes.

John's brother Charles alone wrote over 6,000 new hymns.

In America, the Methodist and Baptist missionaries commonly preached to racially mixed audiences at outdoor camp meetings. These meetings of frontier people, slaves, and African American free people required a different music. Since most couldn't read, simple choruses and spirituals replaced hymnals. A leader "lined out the words," and the congregation repeated them. This style of hymn singing began in the 17th century in the British Isles; the style was similar to the call-and-response songs of the slaves, and it caught on quickly with both races.

Because of the similarities between African American and white spiritual music, **musicologists** have argued over which influenced which. Borrowed elements can be found in both directions, and as the races intermingled in the South, it became impossible to determine the origin of most songs. One song that can be traced back is "Roll, Jordan, Roll":

My brudder sittin' on de tree of life
And he yearde when Jordan roll
Roll, Jordan, roll, Jordan, roll, Jordan, roll!

Little children, learn to fear the Lord,
And let your days be long
Roll, Jordan, roll, Jordan, roll, Jordan, roll!

O let no false no spiteful word
Be found upon your tongue
Roll, Jordan, roll, Jordan, roll, Jordan, roll!

The Negro spiritual borrowed from the hymn sung by Methodist missionaries at camp meetings by Charles Wesley:

He comes, He comes the Judge severe,
Roll, Jordan, roll!
The seventh trumpet speaks him near,
Roll, Jordan, roll!

His lightnings flash, His thunders roll,
Roll, Jordan, roll!
How welcome to the faithful soul,
Roll, Jordan, roll!

Wesley borrowed the tune from a popular 18th-century tune celebrating a British admiral's return to England in victory:

He comes! He comes! The hero comes!
Sound your trumpets, beat your drums!
From port to port let cannons roar
His welcome to the British shore.

Black spirituals arose out of a culture of slavery. White spirituals arose out of life on the frontier. Both racial groups lived a hard life and looked forward to a better time. While both groups shared song themes and melodies, the outlook was far different. Slaves worked together and suffered together under slavery. Pioneer families lived in solitude.

Death always lurked nearby in the early days of the country. Children died of diseases almost unknown today. Antibiotics now provide a sense of security no one experienced before the mid-20th century. Today people successfully avoid thinking about death. In the past it was faced frequently. Songs full of meaning to past generations today sound morbid to us.

For example, many North Americans used to love to sing about blood. The Christian concept of conversion includes the idea that the old sinful self dies and is reborn. Baptism is the symbolic washing away of the old sins. In the Old Testament, sins were removed by animal sacrifice. In the New Testament the sacrifice was through the blood of Christ. The old hymns sing of being "washed in the soul-cleansing blood of the Lamb." It is not a pleasant metaphor for modern people who buy cellophane wrapped meat and avoid blood altogether. Nevertheless "blood" hymns survive.

> There is a fountain filled with blood,
> Drawn from Immanuel's veins;
> And sinners plunged beneath that flood,
> Lose all their guilty stains.
>
> Dear dying Lamb, thy precious blood
> Shall never lose its power,
> Till all the ransomed church of God
> Be saved to sin no more.
>
> Then in a nobler, sweeter song,
> I'll sing thy power to save,

When this poor lisping, stammering tongue
Lies silent in the grave.

This hymn by Isaac Watts was popular in both white and black North American churches. The last two lines of the stanzas are repeated but otherwise it looks like a poem. The following song, an African American spiritual, is completely different. It has lots of repetition and the call-and-response format, an indication that it was not originally written down. The above song ends in death, while the spiritual that follows looks beyond death to the hope of resurrection.

I'm gonna tell you 'bout the coming of the judgment.
Fare thee well, fare thee well.
I'm gonna tell you 'bout the coming of the judgment.
Fare thee well, fare thee well.

There's a better day a coming, fare thee well, fare thee
   well.
Yes there's a better day a coming, fare thee well, fare thee
   well.

Both African and European Americans drew comfort from their faith. Their religion was one of the most important aspects of their lives. Religion made sense out of the hardship and pain they encountered in life. It gave them hope. And these deep feelings inspired countless religious songs that were passed along from group to group. Today, those same songs are a part of our folk heritage.

*Song has played an important part in social protests, uniting and inspiring people to act together.*

# FIVE

## Protest Songs
### We Shall Overcome

*Protest songs helped unite Civil Rights marchers in the 1960s.*

Love, labor, and religion were not the only motivations for singing. People also sang out their rebellion. As they rose up against unjust conditions, songs served to inspire them and give them courage; songs also united them into a single cause.

## UNION SONGS

The Industrial Revolution changed the nature of work and the music that arises out of it. People migrated from the farms and their rural life to the factories. They traded the long, hard hours of farm work with its planting and harvesting for the long, weary hours running huge dangerous machines for low pay.

Working for a large company often created a feeling of powerlessness. As working conditions worsened, workers realized that while they were powerless individually, together they could stop the wheels of industry. They organized unions to bargain for better and safer working conditions, shorter workdays, and higher pay. They gathered at rallies and sang new versions of old songs. The songs emboldened and fortified the will of the workers.

The companies tried discouraging the unions. Fighting broke out, and people were sometimes killed. The martyrs became heroes in songs. Unions gained more sympathy and power. The union movement adopted the folk music style. Today folk music remains an important part of union activities.

Union songs stressed the importance or working together:

"You Gotta Go Down and Join the Union," "Stand Together," "We Belong to the Union." Other songs expressed the sentiments of workers: "I Hate the Company Bosses" and "I'm Proud to Be Union." Still others encouraged union members to support unionized companies: "Don't Forget the Union Label."

Union people took union membership very seriously. This song indicates that union men attract women, but woe to the scab (a worker who doesn't belong to the union or takes the place of striking workers). When it comes to true love, the union comes first!

## THE UNION BOY

When I first arrived in Quirindi those girls they jumped
    for joy,
Saying one unto the other here comes a union boy.

We'll treat him to a bottle and likewise to a dram,
Our hearts we'll freely give too to all staunch union men.

I had not been long in Quirindi not one week two or three,
When a handsome pretty fair maid she fell in love with
    me.

She introduced me to her mother as a loyal union man.
Oh mother, dearest mother, now he's gently joined the
    gang.

Oh daughter, dearest daughter, oh this can never be,
For four years ago, oh he scabbed at Forquadee.

Oh mother, dearest mother, now the truth to you I'll tell.
He's since then joined the union and the country knows
   it well.

Now Fred you've joined the union, so stick to it like
   glue,
For the scabs that were upon your back they're now but
   only few.

And if you ever go blacklegging or scabbing it likewise,
It's with my long, long fingernails I'll scratch out both
   your eyes.

I'll put you to every cruelty, I'll stretch you in a vise,
I'll cut you up in a hay machine and sell you for Chinese
   rice.

Come all you young men, oh wherever you may be,
Oh it's hoist up the flag, oh the flag of unity.

Then scabbing in this country will soon be at an end,
And I pray that one and all of you will be staunch union
   men.

Immigrants from around the world brought their protest songs with them to North America. Many union songwriters often borrowed old melodies rather than invent new ones. The song that follows is sung to the tune of "O Christmas Tree." It was written well before the Bolshevik revolution in Russia. Still, any similarity to the red flag of the old communist Soviet Union is probably not coincidental.

# THE RED FLAG (BY JAMES O'CONNELL, 1899)

The worker's flag is deepest red,
It shrouded oft our martyred dead,
And ere their limbs grew stiff and cold
Their life-blood dyed its every fold.

CHORUS
Then raise the scarlet standard high!
Beneath its folds we'll live and die.
Though cowards flinch and traitors sneer,
We'll keep the red flag flying here.

# THE CIVIL RIGHTS MOVEMENT

All United States citizens are guaranteed equal treatment and protection under the law. In the past, however, some citizens have been "more equal" than others. Segregation was practiced widely in the South. This was a system of laws and customs designed to keep blacks and whites separate. In the South, African Americans were kept from voting by requiring land ownership, the ability to read and write, and the payment of a poll tax for the right to vote. African Americans were barred from certain jobs; they could not **patronize** "whites only" businesses. Black children could not attend white schools.

Black people organized to protest the unfair treatment, but their progress was slow. Then in 1955 one incident **galvanized** blacks all over the country: Rosa Parks refused to move to the back of the bus and sat in the "whites only" front seat. She was arrested. The incident sparked a citywide **boycott** of the bus system—and the civil rights movement was born.

This simple old Baptist hymn became the anthem of the civil rights movement. The melody comes from a pre-Civil War song, "No More Auction Block for Me."

We shall overcome
Oh, deep in my heart
I do believe
We shall overcome someday.

We'll walk hand in hand. . . .

We shall live in peace. . . .

We shall all be free. . . .

We are not afraid. . . .

Singing gave voice to those who had been abused. It expressed their frustration and sorrow—and it gave them courage to fight back against their oppressors.

# MARTIN LUTHER KING, JR.

One of the best-known leaders of the civil right movement was Martin Luther King, Jr. He believed in using nonviolent means to change American society. The descendent of a long line of preachers, King was also a pastor, who used faith in God as a uniting force for African Americans. A powerful leader and **advocate** for African Americans, he inspired African Americans to fight peacefully for their rights. At his rallies, he often used spirituals and other religious folk songs to encourage and unite his listeners.

He was assassinated in 1968.

Today we have romanticized the cowboy's life, but in the 19th century, cowboys were not respected. As the cowboy's life became glamorized by television and movies, their songs gained new popularity.

# SIX

# Cowboy and
# Convict Songs
## From Prairies to Prison

*Few real-life cowboys would have played a guitar, since this instrument would not have been easy to carry with them on horseback.*

IN THE 19TH century, cowboys and convicts were society's outcasts. These groups lived their lives beyond the edge of respectable people's boundaries—and yet cowboys and convicts created a large body of folk songs that people still sing today.

## COWBOY SONGS

The era of the open-range trail drives (from pasturage to pasturage to the railroad) only lasted for approximately 30 years, from the Civil War till about the turn of the century. However, there were cowboys before that—and there are cowboys aplenty still today.

One writer (John Greenway in *Folklore of the Great West*) describes the true cowboy as the top of the lowest **caste** in America. A migrating worker, he was one step above the hobo (an **itinerant** nonworker), and two steps above a bum (a **sedentary** nonworker.) "There wasn't much below the cowboy but the cow."

Cowboys were poorly paid and poorly dressed; their job was simply to drive herds of cattle to distant slaughterhouses near the cities. But time and TV have altered the image of the American cowboy into a romantic **icon** recognized and revered all over the world. Dirty and smelly cattle ropers have been replaced by guitar-strumming crooners in freshly laundered shirts and shiny spurs riding **palomino** horses.

The real cowboys did sing when the work wasn't too long and hard. They would gather around a campfire at night. One would play a harmonica or a banjo—but rarely a guitar, which wouldn't have held up well on long trips.

Cowboys seemed to like soppy sad songs. A lot of the lyrics have to do with dying and loneliness and bad decisions leading to worse consequences:

"Oh bury me not on the lone prairie."
These words came low and mournfully
From the pallid lips of a youth who lay
On his dying couch at the break of day. . .

"Oh bury me not—" and his voice failed there,
But they gave no heed to his dying prayer.
In a narrow grave just six by three,
They buried him there on the lone prairie.

The following song came to America with immigrants from the British Isles. Originally, "The Unfortunate Rake" was a story about a dying Irishman who lived fast and died young. In the Appalachian region it became the song of a dying woman known as "The Bad Girl's Lament." Among Southern African American singers, the song was sung as "St. James Infirmary," the location of the main character's death. In the West, cowboys sang a version of the same song. It was called "The Streets of Laredo" or "The Cowboy's Lament."

As I walked out in the streets of Laredo,
As I walked out in Laredo one day,
I spied a poor cowboy all wrapped in white linen,
Wrapped in white linen as cold as the clay.

"I see by your outfit that you are a cowboy,"
These words he did say as I boldly walked by,
"Come sit down beside me and hear my sad story,
I'm shot in the breast, and I know I must die."

"It was once in the saddle I used to go dashing,
Once in the saddle I used to go gay,
First down to Rosie's and then to the card house,
Shot in the breast and I'm dying today."

# CONVICT SONGS

While the cowboy may dip his toe into the water of bad living, the convict has jumped in headfirst. The convict may even be better off than the poor boy away from his home and out on the range. While prison life might be easier than poverty, the song concludes with the irony of prison comforts:

Corn pone, fat meat,
All I gits to eat.
Better'n I has at home,
Better'n I has at home.

Cotton socks, striped clothes,
No Sunday glad rags at all.
Better'n I get at home,
Better'n I get at home.

Chain gang songs are similar to the work songs sung by slaves during the century before. Most work songs nearly disappeared when machines replaced manual labor. Prisons now became work songs' last resting place. In the work song below, the "huh!" marks the stroke of the pick ax or hammer:

Look over yonder, huh!
Hot burning sun turning over

# LEADBELLY

(Step right up, folks and see a gen-u-ine authentic folk singer!)

As soon as methods of recording were available, musicologists combed the country looking for styles of folk music. The idea was to preserve as much of these precious cultural
artifacts as possible before they were lost forever. The Lomaxes' father-and-son team was
perhaps the most successful of these folk music collectors.

The Lomaxes visited the Angola Prison Farm in Louisiana in 1933 to record songs
sung by the prisoners there. They were particularly impressed by a black prisoner,
Huddy Ledbetter, because of his broad knowledge of folk music, his powerful voice, and
his distinctive style of playing the 12-string guitar. They successfully petitioned the governor for his pardon the next year and hired him as their chauffeur.

Huddie, better known as Leadbelly, was born to sharecropper parents. Little is known
of his youth. As an adult, he was a large, muscular man with a hot temper. He killed a
man in 1917 in a fight over a woman and was sentenced to 30 years hard labor in prison.
He used his musical talent to avoid the hard labor and managed to get a pardon from the
governor after writing a song for him pleading for freedom.

He was convicted and sent to prison a second time in 1930 for assault with intent to
murder in Louisiana, where the Lomaxes "discovered" him a few years later. They took
Leadbelly to New York City, where he met and performed with the professional "folk
singers" of the day: Pete Seeger, Woody Guthrie, Sonny Terry, and Brownie McGhee.
They gathered at union halls and **hootenannies** and sang protest songs in support of various political causes. He recorded for the Library of Congress, Folkways, and other record
companies. In 1949, he died of **Lou Gehrig's disease**.

Leadbelly's life illustrates the **enigma** of the "enlightened" racism of his time. On the
one hand, white people were fascinated with Leadbelly. He encouraged sensationalized
and inaccurate stories of his convictions and prison time and pardons. It gave him a kind
of aura or mystique among urban white folks living a somewhat bland life. In their eyes,
here was a real man who had lived a real dangerous life. People gathered to hear the ex-
con murderer, twice pardoned by governors in two states by "singing for his freedom."

They identified him as one of the downtrodden, those poor people used by the Establishment and kept in poverty.

And yet in spite of his popularity with white folk enthusiasts and champions of the downtrodden, Leadbelly and his wife remained in poverty. On tour with the Lomaxes, Leadbelly sang, chauffeured, and passed the hat at his concerts, barely making ends meet. Even the Lomaxes apparently did not consider him to be the equal of a white person.

As much as Leadbelly did for introducing white audiences to African American music, he never developed a black audience. Shortly after his death, the Weavers, a white group sent his song, "Good Night Irene" to the number-one place on pop charts. Leadbelly's influence on mostly white musicians continues to be felt today.

Look over yonder, huh!
Hot burning sun turning over
And it won't go down,
Oh my Lord, it won't go down.

My little woman, huh!
She keep sending me letters,
My little woman, huh!
Don't know I'm dead
Oh my Lord, I'm worse than dead.

Folk song collectors consider prisons to be some of the richest sources of folk music. The combination of loneliness, long dull hours, hard labor, and a musical tradition unknown in middle and upper class America yields a musical **genre** with memorable melodies and powerful feeling.

*Train wrecks were the inspiration for many folk songs.*

# SEVEN

## Railroad Songs
### Rhythm in the Rails

*From children's stories to folk songs, trains have captured our imagination.*

THE LONESOME sound of the wailing whistle floats through the night air. The chuketa-chuketa-chuketa rhythm of the wheels pounds the rails. Engineers keep one eye on the water pressure gauge and the other on the rails ahead through the long lonely night. Hobos sing and hitch rides across the country in freight cars. Spectacular train accidents occur to passengers and drivers riding toward home or leaving home.

It's not surprising that trains would inspire a whole genre of music. Here are some examples.


## ROCK ISLAND LINE


This train song celebrates the Chicago, Rock Island, and Pacific Railroad. There are many versions. The rhythm is fast and imitates the pumping of the pistons and clatter of steel wheels on steel rails.

CHORUS:
I say the Rock Island Line is a mighty good road,
I say the Rock Island Line is the road to ride.
Oh, the Rock Island Line is a mighty good road,
If you want to ride it, got to ride it like you're flyin'.
Buy your ticket at the station on the Rock Island Line!

I may be right and I may be wrong,
I know you're gonna miss me when I'm gone.

A B C , double X Y Z,
Cat's in the cupboard, but he can't see me.

Jesus died to save our sins,
Glory be to God, we're gonna need him again.

## THE STORY OF CASEY JONES

Casey Jones is the most famous of the hero engineers during the golden age of the railroad. He was a real person, born John Luther Jones in 1864. At fifteen, he became an apprentice to a railroad telegrapher. By 18, he was a fireman and by 26 a fast-freight engineer.

A nondrinker and reliable, he had a good safety record. He took a job running the Cannonball, the fastest passenger train of the Illinois Central Railroad. Up and down the tracks, people knew Casey was at the helm by the sound of the whistle. Casey

Folk songs have no known author; instead, they spread from person to person and are handed down from generation to generation. But sometimes the line between folk songs and composed songs is a blurry one.

"The Wreck of the Old '97" was another train crash song, which also used the tune from "The Ship That Never Returned." In the late 1920s, this folk song was produced by Victor Records and sold a million copies. A few years later, a man named David C. George sued Victor; he insisted that he was the rightful author of the song's lyrics. A long and lengthy court battle followed.

This train crash song used the melody from "The Ship That Never Returned," the ballad of an older tragedy at sea.

On a dark storm mornin' when the snow was a-fallin'
Through the smoke from the old straight stack,
The train pulled out for St. Louis
With her crew that will never come back.

CHORUS:
Sad farewell when we heard the signal
And the brakeman dropped that pin,
And for hours and hours, well, that brakeman waited
For a train that will never pull in.

played the six-note steam whistle like a musical instrument. Casey loved the speed of the modern steam engines.

One day another engineer fell ill. Casey finished the northbound route and volunteered to run the southbound route. The train was running late already. Casey put on all the steam and headed south at perhaps 70 miles per hour.

In Vaughan, Mississippi, two freight trains sat on the sidings, but they were so long, both had cars still hanging out on the main track. The railroad men put out warning markers and figured when the Cannonball came through they'd pull one end of the train out onto the main track. When the Cannonball passed the siding, they'd reverse the train and pull it back onto the siding. Casey could slip right through.

They didn't reckon on Casy's speed. He hit the brakes with a hiss of steam. There wasn't enough room to stop.

"Jump!" Webb, the *fireman* on board the Cannonball shouted. The train had slowed to about 30 miles per hour.

"You jump, I'll stay," Casey answered as he continued to hold the brake. Webb jumped. None of the passengers were seriously injured in the crash—but Casey was killed. Numerous ballads flourished after the 1900 accident and Casey Jones became a folk hero.

Casey Jones might be the most famous of all the train wreck stories, but other train wrecks inspired numerous other folk songs as well. Today, when we hear of a plane crash or other disaster, our first impulse is not usually to turn the event into a song. Perhaps the extensive media coverage relieves our need to process the tragedy musically. But our folk tradition used music as a way to structure human horror, as a way to remember, and eventually as a way to turn even the most awful events into a reason to sing.

*"Someone's in the kitchen with Dinah. . . ."*

Laying the tracks for the trains that crossed North America was hard work, and the workers sang to wile away their time. Here's one train song that every child knows:

I've been working on the railroad, all the livelong day.
I've been working on the railroad, just to pass the time away.
Can't you hear the captain calling? Rise up so early in the morn.
Can't you hear the captain calling, "Dinah blow your horn!"

Dinah, won't you blow,
Dinah, won't you blow,
Dinah, won't you blow your horn?

Someone's in the kitchen with Dinah.
Someone's in the kitchen, I know.
Someone's in the kitchen with Dinah,
Strumming on the old banjo.

Playing fee-fi-fiddlie-i-o,
Fee-fi-fiddlie-i-o-o-o-o,
Fee-fi-fiddlie-i-o,
Strumming on the old banjo.

*"Clementine" pokes fun at tragic love ballads.*

# EIGHT

## Comic Songs
### Laughter and Serious Singing

*"Found a Peanut" is sung to the same tune as "Clementine."*

THOUSANDS OF years ago, people were also probably making up funny songs for the amusement of their friends and family. And today, the practice continues.

Comic songs fall into all categories of songs. Songs of mayhem and death, songs of love, even hymns have their humorous counterparts.

Some comic songs are original. Others are parodies, copies of another work or song performed in the same style or using the same tune, but done in a humorous or *satirical* manner. Someone has written a parody for nearly every popular song ever written, and folk songs that have stood the test of time are often parodied. Sometimes the parody is better known than the original song. For instance, "Clementine" is a frequently parodied song.

> In a cavern, in a canyon,
> Excavating for a mine,
> Lived a miner, forty-niner,
> And his daughter, Clementine.
>
> CHORUS:
> Oh my darling
> Oh my darling
> Oh my darling Clementine
> You are lost and gone forever,
> Dreadful sorry Clementine.

Light she was and like a fairy,
And her shoes were number nine,
Herring boxes without topses,
Sandals were for Clementine.

Drove her ducklings to the water
Every morning just at nine,
Hit her foot against a splinter,
Fell into the foaming brine.

Ruby lips above the water,
Blowing bubbles soft and fine.
But, alas, I was no swimmer,
So I lost my Clementine.

In a churchyard near the canyon,
Where the myrtle does entwine,
There grow roses and other posies,
Fertilized by Clementine.

How I missed her, how I missed her,
How I missed my Clementine,
Till I kissed her little sister,
And forgot my Clementine.

"Clementine" is a parody of the tragic love ballads we discussed
in chapter three. It pokes fun at serious songs of the same nature.

Listen Girl Scouts, heed the warning
To this tragic tale of mine,
Artificial respiration
Could have saved my Clementine.

Sometimes a parody may parody a parody (if you can follow that train of reasoning). For instance, one parody of Clementine is the well known "Found a Peanut":

> Found a peanut, found a peanut
> Found a peanut just now
> Just now I found a peanut, found a peanut just now.

> Cracked it open. . .

> It was rotten. . .

> Ate it anyway. . .

> Got a tummy ache. . .

> Called the doctor. . .

> Gave me medicine. . .

> Died anyway. . .

> Went to Heaven. . .

> Met Saint Peter. . .

. . . and on it goes. The foolishly tragic words are all sung to the tune of "Clementine." Depending on the creativity of the singers, the singer's travels through Heaven and Hell can rival Dante's Divine Comedy in length and breadth.

Humor is one human response to life's tragedies and hard-

Some songs that start out as parodies take on new meaning with time. For instance, in pre-Revolutionary days, the British troops came up with a song that poked fun at the rustic and ill-equipped colonial troops.

Father and I went down to camp,
Along with Captain Gooding;
And there we saw the men and boys,
As thick as hasty pudding.

CHORUS
Yankee doodle, keep it up,
Yankee doodle dandy;
Mind the music and the step,
And with the girls be handy.

There was Captain Washington
Upon a slapping stallion,
A-giving orders to his men,
I guess there was a million.

And then the feathers on his hat,
They looked so tarnal fine-a,
I wanted pockily to get
To give to my Jemima.

And then we saw a swamping gun,
Large as a log of maple;
Upon a deuced little cart,
A load for father's cattle.

And every time they shoot it off,
It takes a horn of powder;
It makes a noise like father's gun,
Only a nation louder.

You may not be familiar with these verses (or the 186 additional verses we've omitted)—but almost everyone knows "Yankee Doodle." A song that was created as a parody ended up being adopted by the American troops; they claimed it as their own. When the British commander Cornwallis surrendered at Yorktown at the end of the Revolutionary War, the American troops sang "Yankee Doodle." Meanwhile, the British troops sang this song:

If buttercups buzzed after the bee,
If boats were on land, churches on sea,
If ponies rode men, and if grass ate the cows,
And cats should be chased into holes by the mouse,
If the mamas sold their babies to the gypsies for half a crown,
If summer were spring and the other way 'round,
Then all the world would be upside down.

*"The World Turned Upside Down"*

ships. Comic songs poke fun at ourselves. They remind us not to take ourselves so serious.

For instance, students have traditionally used humor to help them handle their feelings of rebellion and frustration. Songs by students about teachers are legion:

Row, row, row, your boat
Gently down the stream,
Throw the teacher overboard,
And listen to her scream.

And we've all heard the Chiquita banana song:

I'm Chiquita banana and I'm here to say,
If you want to get rid of your teacher today,
Just peel a banana and throw it on the floor,
And watch your teacher go sliding out the door.

Or how about that all-time favorite, sung to the tune of the "Battle Hymn of the Republic":

Glory, glory, hallelujah!
Teacher hit me with a ruler.
The ruler turned red, and the teacher dropped dead,
And there ain't no school no more!

Bargemen who worked on the Erie Canal also needed a sense of humor. The Erie Canal was 40 feet wide and four feet deep. Running across the northern part of New York State's flat plain, life for the canallers was quite dull. One man kept the barge from scraping the edge while another kept the mule to its task of plodding along the towpath. Every few miles the barge reached a **lock** where the barge was raised or lowered to the next level. The life of

the bargemen was not particularly exciting; the worst dangers on the canal were perhaps other drunken bargeman and mosquitoes. One of the popular songs of canal men pretended they were real sailors. (During the canal days, the word canal was pronounced "canawl." This explains the rhyming of "canal" with "fall.")

## THE RAGING CANAL

The winds came roaring on,
Just like a wild cat scream,
Our little vessel pitched and tossed,
Straining every beam.

The cook she dropped the bucket,
And let the ladle fall,
And the waves ran mountains high
An the raging canal.

The captain came on deck
With spy glass in his hand,
But the fog it was 'tarnel thick,
He couldn't spy the land.

The clouds were all upsot,
And the rigging it did fall
And we scudded under bare poles
On that raging canal.

Folk songs weren't all created long ago in the mists of time. They are still springing up today, and they spread through our culture as they speak to an experience common to many of us.

For instance, today's college students can relate to the comic folk song that follows. Almost all of them have discovered the value of coffee for staying awake to cram for midterm or final exams. The coffee machine at the end of the dormitory hall became a popular gathering spot.

# THE COFFEE MACHINE

Oh! if you have a problem, bring it on to me,
Hand me over one thin dime, and there you are you see.
Your problem's over
You are in clover.
One old cup of black solution
Brings an end to your confusion,
Works just like a blood transfusion!

CHORUS
Coffee machine we love you!
You are our student center.
We put our books above you,
Then listen to our mentor.

*"The Coffee Machine"*

Comic songs can help us handle the frustrations of daily life. Almost all of us, at one time or another, have had to endure the frustration of unappetizing food.

## MRS. MURPHY'S CHOWDER

Won't you bring back,
won't you bring back
Mrs. Murphy's chowder.
It was tuneful

*"Mrs. Murphy's Chowder"*

every spoonful
made you yodel louder.
After dinner, Uncle Ben
used to fill his fountain pen
From a plate of Mrs. Murphy's chowder.

CHORUS
It had ice cream, cold cream, benzene, gasoline,
Soup beans, string beans, floating all around . . .
Sponge cake, beefsteak, mistake, stomachache, cream
    puffs, earmuffs, many to be found.
Silk hats, doormats, bed slats, democrats,
Cowbells, door bells beckon you to dine,

Meatballs, fish balls, mothballs, cannonballs.
Come on in, the chowder's fine!

Won't you bring back, won't you bring back
Mrs. Murphy's chowder?
From each helping you'll be yelping
For a headache powder.
And if they had it where you are,
You might find a trolley car
In a plate of Mrs. Murphy's chowder.
CHORUS

Wont you bring back, won't you bring back
Mrs. Murphy's chowder?
You can pack it, you can stack it all around the larder.
The plumber died the other day.
They embalmed him right away
In a bowl of Mrs. Murphy's chowder.

In "Hush Little Baby," parents promise their children a long list of items, including a billy goat, hoping to bribe the children into sleeping.

# NINE

# Children's Songs

## Why People
## Shouldn't Swallow Flies

*The lyrics of "Rock-A-Bye Baby" are somewhat ominous!*

Young children use music to make sense of the world around them. Songs also help them to learn, since they are easier to remember than rote memorization. Everyone learns the alphabet by the "Alphabet Song." (You don't remember it? Here is the first line to jog your memory: *ABCDEFG. . . .* All you have to do is sing it to the tune of "Twinkle, Twinkle, Little Star."

The first song heard by an infant is the lullaby. These are usually sung by desperate parents, hoping to soothe a squalling or **colicky** child. These songs often promise something to the child if they will only go to sleep:

> Hushaby, don't you cry,
> Go to sleep my little baby.
> When you wake,
> You shall have cake
> And all the pretty little horses. . . .

Various ethnic groups offered their babies different items: a soft fuzzy rabbit skin, a fish, an egg, or a chick. Inexperienced parents, of course, don't realize you can't promise something to a child because they will want it now. The worst song for promising things the parents won't actually deliver is "Hush Little Baby":

> Hush little baby don't say a word.
> Papa's going to buy you a mockingbird.
> If that mockingbird don't sing,

Papa's going to buy you a diamond ring.
If that diamond ring is brass,
Papa's going to buy you a looking glass.
If that looking glass gets broke
Papa's going to buy you a billy goat. . . .

The song runs on in its various versions. One version for the less patient ends with the frustrated parent's threat:

If that billy goat runs away,
Papa's going to spank you on your boom-de-ay.

It's a good thing infants don't understand speech yet. Some songs could give them nightmares. Imagine your parent singing you the horrible song below. (It's no wonder when children do learn the language they file through their unconscious memories while asleep and dream of falling.)

Rock-a-bye baby
On the treetop.
When the wind blows, the cradle will rock.
When the bough bends the cradle will fall,
And down will come baby, cradle and all.

As children get older, they are no longer dependent on their parents for song; now they sing their own songs. Children naturally sing with their whole body, and songs for children often are accompanied by hand motions or games. One simple game for young children involves one child sitting in the center while the others form a ring. The children in the ring sing to one of the

most popular children's tunes, "Here We Go 'Round the Mulberry Bush":

> Lazy Mary, will you get up,
> Will you get up,
> Will you get up,
> Lazy Mary, will you get up,
> Will you get up today?

The child in the center, Lazy Mary, answers:

> No, no Mother, I won't get up,
> I won't get up,
> I won't get up,
> No, no Mother, I won't get up,
> I won't get up today.

At the end of the song, the children in the ring run away as Lazy Mary jumps up and tries to catch one. The child she catches becomes the new Lazy Mary and the game is repeated.

Older children sing longer songs, including songs that accumulate things such as "Old McDonald Had a Farm" or "I Know an Old Lady":

> I know an old lady who swallowed a fly.
> I don't know why she swallowed the fly.
> Perhaps she'll die.

> I know an old lady who swallowed a spider
> That wriggled and jiggled and tickled inside her.
> She swallowed the spider to catch the fly.

I don't know why she swallowed the fly.
Perhaps she'll die.

I know an old lady who swallowed a cat.
Imagine that! She swallowed a cat.
She swallowed the cat to catch the spider
That wriggled and jiggled and tickled inside her.
She swallowed the spider to catch the fly.
I don't know why she swallowed the fly.
Perhaps she'll die.

The song continues in the same vein, with each verse repeating
the animals from the earlier verses:

I know an old lady who swallowed a
   dog.
What a hog to swallow a dog!

. . . a goat.
She just opened her throat and in
   walked the goat.

. . . a cow.
I don't know how she swallowed the
   cow!

She swallowed the cow to catch the
   goat.

*"I Know an Old Lady"*

She swallowed the goat to catch the dog.
She swallowed the dog to catch the cat.
She swallowed the cat to catch the spider
That wriggled and jiggled and tickled inside her.
She swallowed the spider to catch the fly.
I don't know why she swallowed the fly.
Perhaps she'll die.

The tragic end of the song sneaks up on the unwary listener:

I know an old lady who swallowed a horse . . .
She's dead, of course.

Some songs tell stories, include hand motions and even end up with a corny punch line. Bunny Foo Foo is a classic bully. The song is sung to the tune of "Alouette." Italicized lines are spoken.

Little Bunny Foo Foo,
Hopping through the forest.
Scooping up the field mice,
And bopping them on the head.

*And along came a good fairy and she said:*

"Little Bunny Foo Foo,
I don't want to see you,
Scooping up the field mice,
And bopping them on the head.

*I'll give you three more chances.*
*And if you're not good,*

*"Little Bunny Foo Foo"*

*I'll turn you into a goon!"*
*So the next day . . .*

Little Bunny Foo Foo,
Hopping through the forest.
Scooping up the field mice,
And bopping them on the head.

*Along came the good fairy and she said:*

"Little Bunny Foo Foo,
I don't want to see you.

Scooping up the field mice,
And bopping them on the head.

*I'll give you two more chances.*
*And if you're not good,*
*I'll turn you into a goon!"*
*So the next day . . .*

Little Bunny Foo Foo,
Hopping through the forest.
Scooping up the field mice,
And bopping them on the head.

*And along came a good fairy and she said:*

"Little Bunny Foo Foo,
I don't want to see you.
Scooping up the field mice,
And bopping them on the head.

*I'll give you one more chance.*
*And if you're not good,*
*I'll turn you into a goon!"*
*So the next day . . .*

Little Bunny Foo Foo,
Hopping through the forest.
Scooping up the field mice,
And bopping them on the head.

*I gave you three chances to be good,*
*And you didn't behave.*

*And now, I'm going to turn you into a goon*
**POOF**
*The moral of this story is:*
*"Hare today, goon tomorrow."*

Some songs fall into a continuous loop and never end. This song comes from Pennsylvania Dutch country:

"There's a hole in the bucket dear Liza, dear Liza"
There's a hole in the bucket dear Liza, a hole."

"Then mend it dear Henry, dear Henry,
"Then mend it dear Henry, mend it."

"With what shall I mend it dear Liza,
   dear Liza,
With what shall I mend it dear Liza,
   with what?"

"With straw dear Henry, dear Henry,
   dear Henry,
With straw dear Henry, dear Henry,
   with straw."

"With what shall I cut it dear Liza, dear
   Liza,

*"There's a Hole in the Bucket"*

With what shall I cut it dear Liza, with what?"

"With a knife, dear Henry. . ."

"The knife is too dull dear Liza. . ."

"Then sharpen it dear Henry. . ."

"With what shall I sharpen it dear Liza. . ."

"With a stone dear Henry. . ."

"The stone is too dry dear Liza. . ."

"Then wet it dear Henry. . ."

"With what shall I wet it dear Liza. . ."

"With water dear Henry. . ."

"With what shall I fetch it dear Liza. . ."

"With a bucket dear Henry. . ."

"There's a hole in the bucket dear Liza! . . ."

Children love to sing. It's a pleasure few of us outgrow. Radios, CDs, and music videos offer us a commercial avenue for song—but unpublished folk songs will continue to be handed on, from parents to children, from child to child, an everlasting heritage of song.

# Further Reading

*American Folksongs.* New York: Hal Leonard Publishing, 1999.

Doyle, Donnie. *Along Lot Seven Shore: Folksongs and Other Writings.* New York: Acorn Press, 2001.

Lomax, John A. *Our Singing Country: Folk Songs and Ballads.* Mineola, N.Y.: Dover, 2000.

Lomax, John A. and Alan Lomax. *American Ballads and Folk Songs.* Mineola, N.Y.: Dover, 1994.

McNeill, W.K. *Southern Mountain Folksongs: Traditional Folksongs from the Appalachians and the Ozarks.* New York: August House, 1993.

Sandburg, Carl and Garrison Keillor. *The American Songbook.* New York: Harvest Books, 1990.

# For More Information

American Folk Music
www.jdray.com

Folk Music
www.contemplator.com/folk.html

www.acronet.net/~robokopp/English.html

Folk Song Lyrics
Home.t-online.de/home/pheld/texte1a.htm

Folk Songs and Ballads of the Appalachians
www.netstrider.com

Song Lyrics for Kids
www.kididdles.com/mouseum/y004.html

# Glossary

**Advocate**  One who speaks in defense of another.

**Arbitrary**  Determined by individual preference or convenience.

**Boycott**  To refuse to have dealings with a person, store, or organization, in order to express disapproval or to force acceptance of certain conditions.

**Capsulate**  To condense into a brief form.

**Caste**  A division of society based on wealth, profession, or inherited rank or privilege.

**Colicky**  Fussy because of stomach pains.

**Enigma**  A mystery.

**Fireman**  The person who tended the fire on a train engine.

**Galvanized**  Stimulated or excited for action.

**Holler**  "Hollow" or valley.

**Hootenannies**  Gatherings of folksingers where the audience often joined in.

**Icon**  Emblem or symbol.

**Itinerant**  Traveling from place to place.

**Ken**  Know.

**Lou Gehrig's disease**  A rare progressive degenerative disease that affects the spinal cord; it usually begins in middle age and is characterized by spreading muscular weakness.

**Musicologists**  People who study music as a field of research.

**Palomino**  A gold or cream-colored horse.

**Patronize**  To be a frequent or regular customer.

**Repertoire**  The complete list of musical pieces available for performance.

**Satirical**  Using irony or sarcasm.

**Sedentary**  Settled in one place.

**Sledging**  Transporting by means of a strong, heavy sleigh.

**Ubiquitous**  Widespread; constantly encountered.

# Index

# Biographies

Peter Sieling is the owner of Garreson Lumber and the author and publisher of two technical books: *Bee Hive Construction* and *Air Drying Lumber for Maximum Yield.* In addition, he writes for *Bee Culture Magazine.* He enjoys playing the keyboard, harmonica, and banjo. He resides with his wife and three children in upstate New York, where several pea fowls, a goose, approximately 500,000 honeybees, and assorted cats and dogs also keep him company.

Dr. Alan Jabbour is a folklorist who served as the founding director of the American Folklife Center at the Library of Congress from 1976 to 1999. Previously, he began the grant-giving program in folk arts at the National Endowment for the Arts (1974–76). A native of Jacksonville, Florida, he was trained at the University of Miami (B.A.) and Duke University (M.A., Ph.D.). A violinist from childhood on, he documented oldtime fiddling in the Upper South in the 1960s and 1970s. A specialist in instrumental folk music, he is known as a fiddler himself, an art he acquired directly from elderly fiddlers in North Carolina, Virginia, and West Virginia. He has taught folklore and folk music at UCLA and the University of Maryland and has published widely in the field.